DISCRIMINATION AGAINST THE NEGRO

IN AMERICAN ATHLETICS

by

Thomas Elton Foreman

A Thesis

Fresno State College

1957

REPRINTED IN 1975 BY

R AND E RESEARCH ASSOCIATES
4843 MISSION STREET, SAN FRANCISCO 94112
18581 McFARLAND AVENUE, SARATOGA, CA 95070

PUBLISHERS AND DISTRIBUTORS OF ETHNIC STUDIES
EDITOR: ADAM S. ETEROVICH
PUBLISHER: ROBERT D. REED

LIBRARY OF CONGRESS CARD CATALOG NUMBER
74-76466

ISBN
0-88247-340-9

TABLE OF CONTENTS

PREFACE

Americans have become increasingly conscious in recent years of the problems of racial minorities. Much attention has been focused on such matters as segregation in the schools, segregation on public transportation, and inequality of opportunity in the field of employment. Sociologists have made careful and painstaking studies of the factors involved in these problems, and have collected some valuable information.

There is at least one field, however, in which a minority group, the Negro, has encountered strong discrimination but which has had little serious attention from historians or sociologists; the field of sports.

The field of sports is, nevertheless, an important one in the overall picture of race relations in America, if only because it is one in which the issues and individuals are well known to a large number of the American people. One of the phenomenons of Americal life in the last one hundred years has been the tremendous increase in public interest in sporting events, an interest which has made national figures and popular heroes of many men -- as well as a few women -- solely because of their athletic skills.

Whereas, prior to the Civil War there was little organized athletic activity, in the decades following that war baseball emerged as a national pasttime with organized leagues and games which attracted nationwide attention; college football developed into a sport whose games attracted as many as 30,000 spectators; boxing achieved a status in which the recognized champions became national idols to small boys and adults alike; and a number of lesser sports also developed fervent followings.[1]

This sports interest, attendant on a changing economy which gave the average man far more leisure time than he had ever known before, intensified in the twentieth century. In the decade following World War I, wrote historian Foster Rhea Dulles,

> The country appeared sports-crazy, and every reading of the daily paper confirmed it. In 1919 charges of bribe-taking against the Chicago White Sox created more of a stir than similar charges a few years later against members of the President's Cabinet. In 1928 Tilden's debarment from amateur tennis ranks drove election news, the assasination of Mexico's president-elect, and a search for lost aviators in the Arctic off the front pages of the evening newspapers.[2]

Writing about the emotional connotations attached to one sport, boxing, sports writer John Lardner made the following observations:

> There have been periods in American history when the heavyweight boxing champion outranked the President in popular interest. Jack Johnson's impact on popular feeling was sharper than William H. Taft's. Jack Dempsey overshadowed Calvin Coolidge. . . . Major historians do not speak of it, and probably they do well to stick to the more formal aspects of international affairs, but at the popular level, prizefighting has played as strongly as any factor in non-military life on the emotions of nations and races. Feeling was intense in England and America at the time of the Sayers-Heenan fight, between Tom Sayers, Champion of England, and John C. Heenan, the Benicia Boy, of California. French feeling was intense at the time of the Dempsey-Carpentier fight. Feeling among whites against Negroes was high at the time when John L. Sullivan invented the so-called "color line," and at the time when Jack Johnson crossed the line, some years later and won the championship. . . . At all times in the last sixty years, in nearly all parts of the Western world, people have been profoundly stirred by the implications, whatever they may be, of the prizefight and of world boxing supremacy. To bring in the President of the United States once more, it's been proved that the only thing that can match a Presidential speech in radio circulation (and that includes some of Franklin D. Roosevelt's most momentous talks) is a heavyweight championship fight.[3]

With the world of sports having such an influence on the feelings of millions of people, there is good reason to believe that where questions of race relations become involved with sports activities, these questions assume an importance far greater than the mere winning or losing of a game, or a championship.

The successful athlete from a minority group becomes a symbol -- and in many cases an inspiration -- to other members of his own group, and becomes also a symbol to members of the dominant group. Frederick Cozens and Florence Stumpf state in their book, Sports in American Life:

> When a Jewish boxer wins a title, it is a better answer, for many, to the stereotype "Jews are physical cowards" than a lengthy scientific treaties. When Jackie Robinson is selected the most valuable player in the National League for 1949, it is a powerful antidote to another stereotype, that "Negroes are lazy, shiftless, and unreliable."

> In America the word "champion" carries a magical connotation. The champion is the best, the man at the head of the class. When such a coveted title is carried by a member of any minority group, the boost to the morale of that group is incalculable and the blow to discrimination is strong and sure. [4]

A study of discrimination against the Negro in American sports therefore has an importance beyond its interest to the sports fan. As discrimination in sports has faded, discrimination in other walks of life has also waned. Conversely, where there has been a tightening of the barriers against mixed sports competition, it has usually been part of a general effort to strengthen the barriers between the races in other fields of activity as well. Instances of both types of action and reaction will be discussed in the ensuing pages.

The purpose of this paper will be to trace the historical background of color lines in American sports, to show in what manner those color lines have been broken, and to outline, as adequately as possible with the information available, the present situation in this significant field of American activity.

Literature on the subject is not copious. As was noted, few historians or sociologists have given much attention to sports as an important part of American life. Much literature on the subject of sports is extant which has been written for popular consumption and is not marked by scholarliness or historical accuracy. Such sources have not been used in this paper. There have been, however, some books written on the field of sports by authors sincerely interested in historical accuracy, who have done thorough research in their fields before publishing their work. Such sources have been valuable and are quoted without reservation.

The daily newspapers and their files have also provided much information, particularly about recent developments in the area of discrimination against the Negro in sports.

Finally, much first hand information has been gathered through correspondence with various persons who have been able to give information not otherwise available on such matters as current attitudes toward Negro participation in sporting events, and laws governing such participation.

The situations reported in this paper are fluid ones, subject to change from year to year or even from day to day. However, it was felt by the writer that the situations are important enough to warrant investigation and discussion now rather than waiting for that time in the misty future when all things pertaining to the subject shall be settled, and change shall be no more.

Footnotes

[1] Foster Rhea Dulles, America Learns to Play (New York: D. Appleton-Century, 1940), pp. 183-199.

[2] Ibid., p. 356.

[3]John Lardner, <u>White Hopes and Other Tigers</u> (New York: J. B. Lippincott, 1947), pp. 13-16.

[4]Frederick Cozens and Florence Stumpf, <u>Sports in American Life</u> (Chicago: The University of Chicago, 1953), p. 249.

CHAPTER I

THE COLOR LINES

For most of the first half of the twentieth century, as well as for a decade before that, Negroes were barred from participation in a majority of the organized sports in America. They were barred by a series of color lines which were either written rules, "gentlemen's agreements," or merely tacit understandings that Negroes would not be allowed to participate.

Of these color lines, the two best known existed in professional boxing and in organized baseball. Between 1890 and 1946, no Negro was allowed to play on any of the teams in the professional leagues which constitute organized baseball.[1] Between 1887 and 1935, with the exception of a seven-year period from 1908 to 1915, no Negro was allowed to contest for the heavyweight boxing championship of the world in the professional prize ring.[2] When these two color lines were broken, it marked the beginning of the end of segregation in all sports on a nationwide basis.

Neither in baseball nor in boxing did the bar to Negro participants have any legal standing, nor was it ever written into either sport's code of rules. In each case, however much the bar may have reflected the attitudes of a majority of the white participants in the sport, actual drawing of the color line apparently stemmed from the actions of a few dominant individuals, and was perpetuated by unwritten agreement by succeeding generations.

There is no evidence of any significant protest by either white or Negro athletes or sports fans in the period when these color lines were formed, the 1880's and 1890's. It was a period when the attitude of Negro leaders largely reflected the attitude of Booker T. Washington, that Negroes should strive for trade and technical skills, and not aspire to higher goals. It has been said that Washington, in his Atlanta speech of 1895, gave up the Negro's demand for social and political equality in exchange for some measure of financial security.[3] On another occasion Washington wrote that Negroes should give up the unessentials, "and cling only to the essential . . . property, economy, education, and Christian character. To us just now these are the wheat, all else the chaff."[4]

With this as the attitude of the recognized leader of his race, it is small wonder that there was little general concern over the lot of the Negro who aspired to a professional baseball career, or to the heavyweight boxing championship of the world.

Boxing's Color Line

Boxing, during the last century and a half, has known many prominent Negro fighters. The first Americans to win international renown in boxing were two Negroes, Jim Richmond and Tom Molineaux, each of whom fought the English champion, Tom Cribb, in the early part of the nineteenth century.[5] In the late nineteenth and early twentieth centuries, when boxing began to achieve some aura of respectability, there were three Negroes who won world titles in the lighter weight divisions -- George Dixon, Joe Walcott, and Joe Gans.[6]

However, the feeling developed that it would somehow be bad for the white man's prestige if a colored man held the most important boxing title, the heavyweight championship. John L. Sullivan, the first world's heavyweight champion under the Marquis of Queensbury rules, made a public statement in 1890 offering to meet any and all challengers for his title, but adding:

> In this challenge I include all fighters -- first come, first served -- who are white. I will not fight a Negro. I never have and never shall. [7]

Sullivan's statement established a precedent which was followed by his successors to the heavyweight title, James J. Corbett, Robert Fitzsimmons, and James J. Jeffries, from 1892 to 1905. None ever fought a Negro in a championship match, although sports authority John Lardner has stated that when Jeffries retired in 1905, the best heavyweight fighters in the world were the Negroes Jack Johnson, Sam Langford, Sam McVey, and Joe Jeanette. [8]

Following Jeffries' retirement, the championship was awarded to Marvin Hart. Hart soon lost it to a Nova Scotian, Noah Brusso, who fought under the name Tommy Burns. In the course of defending the title, Burns traveled to Australia and there, on December 26, 1908, he fought the Negro, Jack Johnson. Johnson gave Burns such a thorough beating that the police halted the bout in the fourteenth round. [9]

The victory of the Negro in this bout caused dismay to white sports fans in this country. Search began at once for a white man to win the title back for the white race, and a new phrase, "White Hope," entered the sports language. [10]

Public rancor against Johnson reached its peak after the Negro easily defeated former champion James Jeffries on July 4, 1910. Newspaper accounts of the fight relate not only how easily Johnson defeated Jeffries, but also the contemptuous manner in which he did it, subjecting Jeffries, his seconds, and ringside spectators to a stream of taunts and jibes. [11]

The public reacted explosively. The New York Herald headline for the following day said: "Half Dozen Dead as Crowds Attack Negroes; Reign of Terror Here."[12] Writing more than twenty years later, James P. Dawson, boxing editor of the New York Times, said:

> The yellowing newspaper files record the wild disorder throughout the country which followed Johnson's knockout victory over Jeffries. . . . Racial feeling ran high in advance of the match, and exploded into riots in various sections of the nation in its wake.
>
> It was on this very feeling that Rickard (Tex Rickard, promoter of the fight) capitalized. But the battle aftermath had a salutary effect. Rickard thereafter shunned "mixed" matches for the heavyweight title, although he promoted them frequently in the lighter divisions. Indeed, the promoter frequently confided to me that his fear of the repercussions in no small measure influenced his failure later to arrange a match between Dempsey and Harry Wills, for which a clamor had been created during Dempsey's reign as champion and which unquestionably was the most lucrative bout available when the demand was hottest.[13]

A further result of the Jeffries-Johnson fight was the passage of a law by Congress prohibiting the interstate shipment of motion pictures of prize fights. This was designed to prevent the further displaying of the white man's humiliation, particularly before southern audiences. The law, passed by the 62nd Congress in 1912, declared that:

> It shall be unlawful to send or receive, by mail, railway express, water service, or in any other manner, from any state, territory, or the District of Columbia to any other state, territory, or the District of Columbia, or to bring into this country from any foreign country, any film or other pictorial representation of any prize fight or encounter of pugilists, under whatever name, or any record or account of betting on the same. Any person violating the provisions of this act shall be punished by imprisonment for not exceeding one year or a fine of not exceeding one thousand dollars, at the discretion of the court.[14]

Discussion of the bill in Congress made no direct reference to the Jeffries-Johnson fight, but the racial feelings behind the measure appeared in several passages. On July 1, 1912, in the House, Representative Thetus W. Sims of Tennesse urged that the bill (Senate Bill 7027) be called up because of an impending fight between a Negro and a white man to be held in New Mexico on July 4, but no action could be taken because there was no quorum present. [15]

In discussion in the House on July 10, Congressman S. A. Roddenberry of Georgia said:

> I call the attention of the House to the fact that the recent prize fight which was had in New Mexico presented, perhaps, the grossest instance of base fraud and bogus effort at a fair fight between a Caucasian brute and an African biped beast that has ever taken place. It was repulsive. This bill is designed to prevent the display to morbid-minded adults and susceptible youth all over the country of representations of such a disgusting exhibition. [16]

Mr. William G. Sharp of Ohio had this question for the Georgia Congressman:

> I wish to ask the gentleman if he thinks it more indefensible for a white man and a black man to engage in a prize fight than for two white men to engage in such a conflict? [17]

Mr. Roddenberry replied:

> The act as a matter of moral conduct is the same. It differs in degree. No man descended from the old Saxon race can look upon that kind of a contest without abhorrence and disgust. [18]

The bill was signed by President Taft on July 31[19] and remained effective for more than a decade. [20]

Although the probabilities are that he was not conscious of the fact, Johnson's winning of the heavyweight boxing championship coincided with a general movement on the part of Negro leaders in the United States to break away from the pattern of social docility set by Booker T. Washington in the previous century. The founding of the Boston Guardian by Monroe Trotter in 1901, presaging the growth of a Negro press of militant protest;[21] the launching of the Niagara Movement in 1905 by W. H. DuBois;[22] the founding of the National Association for the Advancement of Colored People in 1910;[23] and the beginning of the National Urban League in 1911[24] all occurred during his active career. In

his own way, Johnson was an embodiment of this new spirit of protest. A proud and arti-

culate man, he refused to accept the badge of inferiority either as a fighter or as a human

being. His actions gave white supremacists new ammunition in their contention that a

Negro should not be allowed to hold such an eminent position as heavyweight champion of

the world. He even flaunted the prime bugaboo of the racist, miscegenation. Of this

phase of Johnson's character, John Lardner wrote:

> It seems to have been largely because Johnson displayed his tastes
> and appetites frankly, and insisted that his privileges were equal to those
> of any white athlete, that he was denouced, from the time of the Jeffries
> fight on, in print, in pulpits, and in the meetings of uplift societies. (Sev-
> eral conservative Negro clergymen joined in the outcry.) Before long, one
> of Johnson's frank tastes -- for the company of white women -- provided a
> working weapon against him. After his first wife divorced him, he married
> a white woman from Brooklyn. She committed suicide in Chicago a short
> time later. In the fall of 1912, Johnson was indicted by a Chicago federal
> jury for violation of the Mann Act: he was accused of transporting a white
> girl, Lucille Cameron, who had been employed by Johnson as a secretary,
> across a state line for immoral purposes. Miss Cameron was subpoenaed
> as the government's principal witness, but she married Johnson before the
> trial and so disqualified herself from testifying. (The marriage lasted some
> years.) Johnson was convicted anyway, on other testimony, and sentenced
> to a year and a day in prison . . . .

> After the trial, Johnson jumped his bail of fifteen thousand dollars and
> fled to Europe, by way of Montreal . . . . He remained a fugitive till 1920.
> The men who fought him in the interval had to go abroad to find him.[25]

Johnson eventually lost the title to a white man, Jess Willard, in Havana, Cuba,

in 1915. Pictures which show him taking the count of ten while shielding his eyes from

the sun[26] give credence to his later claim that he "laid down" (pretended to be knocked

unconscious), although not necessarily to his contention that he was bribed to do so, with

the further promise that if he surrendered the championship, the Mann Act charge against

him would be dismissed.[27]

If such a promise was made, it was not kept, for on his return to the United States, in 1920, Johnson was put in Leavenworth Prison, where he served all but a few days of his sentence. [28]

When Jack Dempsey won the championship from Willard in 1919, he first stated to the press that he would not fight a Negro. [29] He later changed his mind, or at least his public statement, saying that he would fight any man, regardless of race or color. [30] In spite of this avowal, a proposed match between Dempsey and Negro challenger Harry Wills, as noted previously, never materialized, and it was to be another fourteen years before a Negro would be given a chance to fight for the heavyweight title.

In 1934, Joseph Louis Barrow, whose fighting name was shortened to Joe Louis, appeared on the national scene as an outstanding heavyweight boxer. By this time, memory of the rancor created by Jack Johnson as champion was dim, but there were still those who feared repercussions should Louis, an Alabama-born Negro, become world champion. Describing the scene at ringside of New York's Yankee Stadium when Louis fought Max Baer, generally regarded as the outstanding white fighter of the time, in the fall of 1935, Jonathan Mitchell wrote:

> [The announcer] is bawling into a microphone: "Although Joe Louis
> is colored, he is a great fighter, in the class of Jack Johnson and the
> giants of the past. American sportsmanship, without regard to race,
> creed, or color, is the talk of the world. Behave like gentlemen, whoever
> wins." Nearly two thousand police at the entrances of the Stadium are there
> to break up a possible race riot. [31]

There was, however, no race riot when Louis won that fight, nor when he won the title the following year, defeating James J. Braddock in Chicago. There was no untoward incident during the twelve years he held the championship.

Much was made, while Louis was champion, of his "good behavior" and discretion in representing his race in the public eye. Actually, Louis is a modest and self-contained man by nature, who has led pretty much the kind of life he prefers. His deliberate concessions to prejudice have been few.[32]

Because Louis was an outstanding fighter, and because his personal life was exemplary, virtually any lingering feeling that it was improper for a Negro to be recognized as the world's best prize fighter had vanished by the time he relinquished the title in 1948. The fact that three of his four successors to the heavyweight championship have been Negroes has raised no protests from present-day descendants of the old Saxon race. Except for certain areas in the South where mixed bouts, between Negroes and white men, are prohibited, the color line against the Negro in professional boxing has vanished.

Baseball's Color Line

At its inception as a national sport, baseball had a color line, as the National Association of Baseball Players, formed in 1867, formally excluded Negroes in its articles of incorporation.[33] However, this loosely-knit organization gave way in 1876 to the National Baseball Association, the parent body of what is now known as organized baseball, and this group had no color ban.[34]

In the early 1880's there were approximately twenty Negroes on minor league baseball teams, and two on what was then a major league team, Toledo in the American Association.[35] These were Moses (Fleet) Walker, a catcher, and his brother, Welday Walker, an outfielder. The names and playing records of both are listed in The Encyclopedia of Baseball, the game's official record book.[36] There was no protest against their playing until late in the 1884 season, when Richmond, Virginia, acquired a franchise in the American Association. Four Richmond citizens then dispatched the following letter to the Toledo Manager, Charles H. Norton:

Richmond, Virginia
September 5, 1884

Manager, Toledo Baseball Club
Dear Sir:

We, the undersigned, do hereby warn you not to put up Walker, the
Negro catcher, the days you play in Richmond, as we could mention the
names of seventy-five determined men who have sworn to mob Walker
if he comes on the ground in a suit. We hope you will listen to our words
of warning, so there will be no trouble, and if you do not, there certainly
will be. We only write this to prevent much bloodshed, as you alone can
prevent.

Bill Frick
James Kendrick
Dynx Dunn
Bob Roseman[37]

The threat had the desired effect. The Toledo manager did not use either of the

Walkers in any games in Richmond, and at the end of the 1884 season the two Negroes

were dropped from the team.[38]

A man prominent in baseball history, Adrian Anson, manager and first baseman

of the Chicago team in the National League, also contributed to the exclusion of Negroes

from baseball. In 1882 he protested the use of Moses Walker by Toledo in an exhibition

game with his Chicago team, but his protest was ignored by Toledo.[39] In 1887 he protested

so vigorously to the proposed purchase by New York of the National League of a Negro

pitcher, George Stovey, that the deal was not consummated.[40] In the same year he re-

fused to let his team take the field against a Newark team which included two Negroes on

its roster.[41]

Anson's actions and such incidents as the Richmond letter set a precedent which

gradually extended through baseball, until, in 1890, Harrisburg, Pennsylvania, dropped

the last Negro players in organized baseball from its team in order to gain admission to the Atlantic Association. In 1891 there were no Negroes in organized baseball.[42]

In almost all cases the exclusion of Negroes from baseball was by the "unwritten law" or "gentleman's agreement." However, one league did put the color barrier in writing, temporarily. In 1888 the Tri-State League, composed of teams in Illinois, Indiana, and Ohio, adopted a rule to prohibit colored players from performing on any league teams. Negro baseball player Welday Walker wrote to the league president: "The law is a disgrace to the present age and casts derision on the law of Ohio that says all men are equal. . . . I would suggest that your honorable body, in case the law is not repealed, pass one making it criminal for a colored man or woman to be found in a ball ground." The segregation rule was immediately repealed.[43]

Even without written rules, however, the force of the "unwritten law" proved too difficult for the Negro to counteract. From 1890 until 1946, no Negro played on any professional team which was under the jurisdiction of the national organization.[44]

During this period, Negro baseball players had to be content with playing on their own all-Negro teams, which played exhibition games and eventually formed a loosely-knit league. That members of these Negro teams were capable of playing major league baseball, and that some white baseball players found nothing repugnant in playing against Negroes, is attested by the fact that it was a common practice for white major league players to meet Negro teams in exhibition games after the regular season. In 1915 the Lincoln Giants, a Negro team, defeated the National League champion Philadelphia team twice in exhibition games, causing the National League to adopt a ruling that no more than four members of any one major league team could play together in postseason games. In this way the prestige of the big league teams was protected.[45]

One attempt to break the organized baseball color line by subterfuge was made by a major league manager, John McGraw, in 1901. He hired a Negro star, Charles Grant, for his Baltimore team and attempted to pass Grant off as an American Indian. However, when Grant made his first appearance in the Baltimore lineup his Negro fans gave him such an ovation that the deception was revealed and McGraw was ordered to get rid of the Negro, by league officials. He complied.[46]

During the 1930's an occasional sports column or magazine article decried the fact that baseball, supposed to be the "great American pasttime," was denying a large segment of the American population a chance to participate. However, it was not until the 1940's that any concrete action was taken to break the color line.

When such action was taken, it was but a part of a general movement which occurred in the 1940's for equality of employment opportunities for Negroes. To a large extent this movement was stimulated by World War II, and the fact that large numbers of Negro citizens were being called on to fight and die for what Americans liked to believe was a democratic way of life. The world conflict quickened the consciences of many whites; the inconsistency of waging war against the Nazi theory of the Master Race abroad while denying racial equality at home was obvious. Moreover, the injustice of demanding from Negroes the full obligation of citizenship in the way of military service while deny-ing them many of its privileges became clear to more and more Americans.[47]

A major victory for the Negroes was won when President Roosevelt on June 25, 1941, issued Executive Order 8802. In part this declared:

> . . . the policy of the United States [is] to encourage full participation in the national defense program by citizens of the United States, regardless of race, creed, color, or national origin, in the firm belief that the demo-cratic way of life within the Nation can be defended successfully only with the help and support of all groups within its borders.[48]

What made this more than a mere statement of principle was the appointment of a

Fair Employment Practices Committee (FEPC) to investigate complaints and to take steps

to redress grievances. The FEPC conducted numerous public hearings and focused

publicity on employers and unions which practiced discrimination. At the same time, war

production created a great demand for labor of all kinds, so that between 1940 and 1944

the number of Negroes employed in manufacturing and processing increased from 500,000

to around 1,200,000; in government service from 60,000 to 200,000.[49]

Although President Truman's proposal to continue the FEPC as a permanent post-

war agency was defeated by the filibustering tactics of Senator Theodore Bilbo of Missi-

ssippi and other Southern legislators, similar legislation was put into effect on the state

and city level in several sections of the country. In New York State the Ives-Quinn Anti-

discrimination Act was passed by the state legislature and signed by Governor Thomas

E. Dewey in 1945, and similar measures were enacted in other states and municipali-

ties.[50]

While such measures had no direct effect on baseball, since one of the game's

fundamental principles is that club owners and managers have the right to employ players

according to their own standards of ability, whatever those standards may be, they did

coincide with, and may have inspired, several attempts by various groups and individuals

to do something toward breaking baseball's color line.

On May 16, 1939, New York State Senator Charles D. Perry, a Democrat, of New

York City, introduced a resolution into the state senate disapproving of discrimination

by major league baseball against colored players.[51] No action was taken on the resolu-

tion at that time, and Senator Perry introduced it again on January 22, 1940. Again no

action was taken.[52]

On July 28, 1942, the management of the Pittsburgh team in the National League announced they would give Negro players tryouts,[53] and on September 1, 1942, the management of Cleveland in the American League announced the same thing.[54] However, neither team took any further action along this line.

A resolution passed by the New York Council of the Congress of Industrial Organization on July 29, 1942, condemned organized baseball for its discrimination.[55] When Kenesaw M. Landis, commissioner of baseball, was asked what action he planned to take in regard to this resolution, he replied that it was up to the individual teams in baseball whether or not they used Negroes.[56]

On November 30, 1943, New York City councilman Benjamin J. Davis, Jr., a Negro, offered a resolution asking that organized baseball reconsider its policy toward Negroes. The motion was tabled for further study.[57]

On May 1, 1945, Councilman Davis again introduced a resolution into the council, this time calling on the State Commission on Discrimination to investigate organized baseball for possible violation of the Ives-Quinn Law. This motion was also tabled, since the Commission had already shown an awareness of the situation in baseball.[58]

This awareness had been shown when a representative of the Commission on Discrimination had approached the presidents of the three New York major league teams, the New York Giants, the New York Yankees, and the Brooklyn Dodgers, asking them to sign a pledge not to discriminate against any player because of his color. Horace Stoneham of the New York Giants indignantly replied that no one could dictate his team's policy in signing players. The commissioners did not press the point.[59]

In April, 1945, a Boston councilman, Isadore Muchnick, used the threat of an ordinance banning Sunday baseball in Boston as a lever to persuade the Boston Red Sox to give tryouts to three Negro players. The Red Sox went through the motions of giving the three, Sam Jethroe, Marvin Williams, and Jackie Robinson, a thorough tryout, then told them they would let them know if they were interested in them further. None of the three took the tryout seriously at any time, nor had any expectation of getting into organized baseball as a result of it. [60]

A few days later David Low, the sports editor of the New York Daily Worker, brought Negroes Terris McDuffie and Dave (Showboat) Thomas to the Brooklyn Dodger training camp and demanded that they be given a chance to try out. The Dodger management acceded, but expressed no interest. This was understandable, since the players were respectively 32 and 34 years old, ages when a baseball player is considered well past his prime. [61]

On April 24, 1945, United States Representative in Congress Vito Marcantonio of New York City stated that he planned to introduce a resolution into Congress demanding an investigation of organized baseball for possible violation of anti-trust legislation unless Negroes were permitted to play. [62] This resolution, apparently, did not materialize, since a study of the Congressional Record for that session reveals no mention of it.

On May 3 Albert B. Chandler, who had succeeded Kenesaw M. Landis as commissioner of baseball, said in reply to a question at a press conference, that he would welcome discussion of the problem by any interested parties. He emphasized, as had Landis, that his office had no power to compel any team to use any player against its will. [63]

In April, 1945, a group of New York Negro and white baseball fans, including dancer Bill Robinson, formed an "End Jim Crow in Baseball" committee which picketed Yankee Stadium at the opening game. [64] New York's mayor, Fiorello LaGuardia, announced as a countermeasure that he was forming a civic committee to study the problem and take whatever action was possible. [65]

While all this had been going on, Branch Rickey, then president of the Brooklyn Dodgers organization in the National League, had quietly been making his own plans to bring Negroes into organized baseball. As early as 1943 Rickey had begun scouting the Negro leagues. Arthur Mann, the traveling secretary for the Brooklyn baseball organization at that time, says:

> This was not primarily a long-range sociological move by Rickey, although he was conscious of the sociological importance of the move. His primary motive was to obtain better ball players. [66]

Rickey's investigation convinced him that a Negro athlete named John Roosevelt Robinson, better known as "Jackie" Robinson, was the best prospect to break the baseball color barrier. In the summer of 1945 he talked with Robinson, and gave him a contract to play for the Montreal team in the Brooklyn system in the 1946 season.

In choosing Robinson as a pioneer in this attempt to break a tradition more than sixty years old, Rickey was influenced by factors other than Robinson's native athletic ability, great though that was. Equally important was the fact that Robinson was a college man who had won national fame in football, basketball, and track as well as baseball while at Pasadena Junior College and the University of California at Los Angeles. As such, he was already experienced in mixed athletic competition among white and Negro players, and had encountered some of the prejudices which could be expected to confront him in baseball. [67]

In addition, Rickey had further assured himself that Robinson would be able to stand up under the psychological and social pressure he would be under when, during his long interview prior to signing the Negro to a contract, he had discussed and dramatized some of the unpleasant episodes which might be expected. [68]

The signing of a Negro to play for a team in organized baseball was kept secret until the end of the 1945 season. On October 24, Hector Racine, the president of the Montreal team, made the announcement to the newspapers and the story immediately captured national attention.

Reactions were varied, with many baseball figures expressing approval but others voicing the belief that the experiment just would not work. Horace Stoneham of the New York Giants said, "That's really a fine way to start the program," and added that his own organization would begin investigating the possibility of using Negro players.[69] Conversely, Clark Griffith, president of the Washington Senators, said he did not believe organized baseball had any right to sign players from the Negro leagues.[70] However, T. Y. Baird, owner of the Kansas City Negro team for which Robinson had been playing, gave full approval to the signing of Robinson by Brooklyn.[71]

Rogers Hornsby, a long time major league player and manager, disapproved of the move, saying it would be difficult for a Negro to become a part of a closeknit group such as an organized ball club.[71a]

While many sports writers in southern states shared the opinion of Jack Horner of the Durham, North Carolina News, that "The Negro ball player will soon find himself so uncomfortable, embarrassed, and out of place in organized baseball that he will get out of his own accord,"[72] other southern writers expressed approval of the move.

W. N. Cox of the Norfolk, Virginia, Virginian-Pilot, wrote, "I guarantee that if Jack Robinson hits homers and plays a whale of a game for Montreal the fans will soon lose sight of his color."[73] Smith Barrier, of the Greensboro, North Carolina, Sun, wrote, "I don't see anything wrong with the signing of Jackie Robinson."[74] Hugh Germinio, of the Durham, North Carolina, News, wrote, "If a colored player is good enough to make the major leagues, then I want to see him have that opportunity."[75]

In spite of the adverse predictions that he would not be able to stand the social pressures of his position, Robinson had a successful season with Montreal in 1946. He won the league batting championship, had the best fielding average among second basemen, and was named the most valuable player at the end of the season.[76]

Robinson was promoted to the Brooklyn major league team in 1947, and his play during that season was good enough to win him the award as "Rookie of the Year" in the National League.[77]

Not all baseball men gave up the color line without a struggle, however. There were several attempts to prevent Robinson's playing major league baseball.

In their annual league meeting in January, 1946, the presidents of the National League teams approved a report, an amendment to which read, in part, that ". . . however well intentioned, the use of Negro players would hazard the physical properties of baseball."[78]

According to Branch Rickey, all copies of the report were then taken up by National League president Ford Frick. When Rickey later asked to see a copy, he was told they had all been destroyed.[79] Nothing was said of this publicly until two years later when, in an address at Wilberforce University on February 17, 1948, Rickey told the story of what happened.[80] League officials denied the story, but Rickey stoutly maintained that it was true.[81]

While Robinson was in spring training with the Brooklyn team in 1947, there was some talk among the players of circulating a petition to Rickey that Robinson be kept off the team. Rickey got word of this before any action had been taken and called the ringleaders in one at a time to talk to them. He told each of them that any man who did not care to play on the same team with Robinson would be traded to another team or sent to the minor leagues. There was no further trouble on the Brooklyn team.[82]

Shortly after the 1947 season started, Brooklyn was scheduled for three games in Philadelphia. Bob Carpenter, the president of the Philadelphia team, called Rickey and told him the Philadelphia players would not take the field if Robinson were to play. Rickey promptly replied, "Fine. Then we'll win those three games by forfeit, and the way things are going, we can use those wins." The Philadelphia players took the field as scheduled.[83]

The most serious attempt to preserve the color line was revealed by Stanley Woodward, the sports editor of the New York Herald-Tribune, who on May 8, 1947, "broke" a story that a few days earlier the members of the St. Louis team had threatened to instigate a general players' strike against Robinson's playing. According to Woodward's story, National League president Ford Frick had heard of the proposed strike and had taken prompt action. In a statement to the St. Louis players, he said:

> If you do this, you will be suspended from the league. You will find that the friends you think you have in the press box will not support you, that you will be outcasts. I do not care if half the league strikes. Those who do it will encounter quick retribution. All will be suspended, and I don't care if it wrecks the National League for five years. This is the United States of America, and one citizen has as much right to play as another.[84]

St. Louis officials denied Woodward's story, but Frick admitted that there had been some trouble, but nothing of a really serious nature.[85]

From that time on, the only protests against Robinson's presence in organized baseball came in the form of verbal abuse from some fans and rival players, and occasional incidents in which a rival pitcher may have thrown the ball unnecessarily close to Robinson's head, or a base runner slid toward him with his spikes unusually high.

In accepting such incidents with calmness and restraint, Robinson lived up to the promise he made to Branch Rickey before first signing a contract. Ironically, in doing so he incurred some displeasure from members of his own race.

Robinson's problem was a basic one, which Negro leaders in all walks of life have had to face, and to which no easy solution has been worked out. In conducting himself with calmness and restraint on the field, even though by nature he is a fiercely competitive athlete whose natural impulse was to fight back when he was insulted or abused, he was guilty in the eyes of some Negroes of being an "Uncle Tom."[86] These Negroes, representing the militant attitude which completely rejects Booker T. Washington's spirit of passive docility, contended that there was no reason why Robinson should not, from the first, have had as much right to argue with an umpire, or to return in kind any physical roughing up as any white player.[87] To them, Robinson was still settling for less than equality as a baseball player.

Robinson, and his sponsor, Branch Rickey, held to the opposite attitude, that the end justified the means, and that by behaving as he did, Robinson made it possible for Negroes to be accepted in organized baseball. Once that acceptance was established, Negro players were free to act like any others. Robinson himself, after three seasons in the major leagues, was given free rein, and became known as one of the most militant players in the league. He was ejected from several games by umpires for disputing their decisions too vigorously, and became involved in many arguments, some of which developed into fights, with rival players.[88] In this he was acting in no way differently from countless white players in baseball history.

At any rate, once the color line was broken, other teams began to use Negro players. Cleveland signed the first Negro ever to play in the American League, Jerry Doby, on July 3, 1947.[89] New York and Boston in the National League began using

Negroes in 1948, and within the next five years, more than half of the teams in the major

leagues had signed Negro players.[90]

The Tennis Situation

Prior to 1950 no Negro had ever been invited to play in the national tennis cham-

pionships at Forest Hills, Long Island. Negroes had been competing in their own American

Tennis Association since its formation in 1917[91] but none of their champions had ever been

given a chance to try his mettle in top flight tournament play.

In 1948 Dr. Reginald Weir, a New York physician and one of the leading Negro

tennis players, entered the National Indoor Tournament, one of the few large scale

tournaments which at that time was open to all contestants, but his showing was unim-

pressive.[92] In 1950, however, a Negro girl, Althea Gibson, entered the National Indoor

Tournament and made a very good showing, reaching the final round. Speculation began

as to what Miss Gibson might do at Forest Hills if she were invited to play, and what her

chances of being invited were.

Former woman tennis star Alice Marble, in an editorial in American Lawn Tennis

magazine, discussed the situation in blunt language. Miss Marble said that she had asked

a member of the national tournament committee about Miss Gibson's chances of being

accepted in the championship tournament, and that the committee member had replied

that Miss Gibson would first have to prove herself in some of the major eastern tourna-

ments. These were all invitational. Asked if he thought the Negro girl would be invited

to play in any of these tournaments, the committee member said he did not think so.

Miss Marble concluded, "Miss Gibson is over a very cunningly wrought barrel, and I can

only hope to loosen a few of its staves with one lone opinion."[93]

Continuing, she said, "I think it's time we face a few facts. If tennis is a game

-20-

for ladies and gentlemen, it's also time we acted like gentle people and less like sancti-

monious hypocrites." Admitting that she did not know how well Miss Gibson might do in

the national tournament, she pointed out that the only way to find out how well the Negro

girl could do would be to give her a chance to play. "But if she is refused a chance to

succeed or fail," said Miss Marble, "then there is an ineradicable mark against a game

to which I have devoted most of my life."[94]

Finally, Miss Marble concluded, "If the field of sports has got to pave the way

for all of civilization, let's do it."[95]

This ringing editorial by one of America's leading tennis figures has been gener-

ally credited with leading the way for Miss Gibson to participate in the national tournament

in 1950. Walter White, secretary of the National Association for the Advancement of

Colored People, was one who so credited Miss Marble.[96]

When Miss Gibson was invited to the English tennis championship tournament at

Wimbledon in 1951[97] the acceptability of Negroes in championship tennis competition

was more firmly assured. Since that time Miss Gibson has competed in all of the major

tournaments, winning several. No other Negro has had her success as yet, but the

magazine Our Sports in 1953 reported that many Negro youngsters are now taking up ten-

nis for the first time, with assurance that they will be allowed to win whatever honors

their ability entitles them to.[98] Further inspiration for aspiring Negro tennis players

was provided this year when Miss Gibson won the Wimbledon women's singles champion-

ship, one of the most coveted titles in tennis, and was presented to Queen Elizabeth

following her victory.[99]

The Crusade in Bowling

In the sport of bowling, a successful crusade against a by-law of the American Bowling Congress, better known as the A.B.C., prohibiting Negro participation in A.B.C. tournaments was carried out between 1946 and 1950.

The United Auto Workers of America adopted a resolution condemning the A.B.C. for discrimination in 1946.[100] In 1948 a National Committee for Fair Play in Bowling was set up, with Mayor Humphrey of Milwaukee and Miss Betty Hicks as co-chairmen. Former Senator James Mead, Philip Murray, and Walter Reuther were others on the committee. Dr. Jay Nash of New York University termed the committee a "torch bearer of a great ideal."[101]

In 1949 the Wisconsin Human Rights Board urged a state ban on the A.B.C. tournament for barring Negroes.[102] In the same year the Congress of Industrial Organization took up the cudgel against the A.B.C., urging that its national charter be revoked.[103] In January, 1950, the Wisconsin State Attorney General attempted to get a court ban on the bowling congress to prevent its national tournament being held in Wisconsin.[104] Shortly after this, the bowling group announced that the ban against Negroes was being dropped.[105]

Action in Other Sports

In other sports, similar action was taken. Late in 1949 Columbia University withdrew its fencing team from the Amateur Fencers League after the league had asked the University to bar two Negro members from league tournaments.[106] Eight days later the league reversed its stand and announced that the Negroes would be allowed to participate.[107]

Another racial bar was broken in 1950 when Dr. R. E. Clarke became the first

Negro to participate in the Grand American Trapshooting Meet, held in Ohio.[108]

In 1948 Manhattan College withdrew from a national college basketball tournament in Kansas City, Missouri, because of a ban on Negro players, and the ban was rescinded two days later.[109]

Golf's Color Line

One of the last major sports to have a national color ban was golf. This was brought to the public's attention in 1952 when the former boxing champion, Joe Louis, sought to enter the San Diego Open Golf Tournament. He was told that the rules of the Professional Golf Association did not allow Negroes to play in P.G.A. sponsored events.[110]

Louis issued a bitter denunciation of the P.G.A., and of its president, Horton Smith, calling the latter "another Hitler."[111] His sentiments were widely echoed by sports writers, golfers, and fans. Smith promised to see what could be done about having the rule changed. A few days later he announced that he had polled the members of the P.G.A. Board of Directors individually, and that they had all agreed to rescind the rule against Negro players in P.G.A. sponsored tournaments.[112]

This action by the national governing body for professional golf removed the last nationwide color line in American sports. From that time on, the fight against racial barriers became one of isolated and individual skirmishes. These are still going on, and some of the significant happenings of recent years will be discussed in the following chapter.

Footnotes

[1] Lee Allen, 100 Years of Baseball (New York: Bartholomew House, 1950), p. 283.

[2] John Lardner, White Hopes and Other Tigers (New York: J. B. Lippincott, 1947), pp. 20-21.

[3] Arnold M. Rose, The Negro's Morale (Minneapolis: University of Minnesota Press, 1949), p. 28.

[4] Booker T. Washington, The Future of the American Negro (Boston: Small, Maynard, 1902), p. 132.

[5] Frank G. Menke, The New Encyclopedia of Sports, (New York: A. S. Barnes, 1947), p. 739.

[6] Roi Ottley, Black Odyssey, (New York: Charles Scribner's Sons, 1950), p. 205.

[7] Donald Chidsey, John the Great, (Garden City: Doubleday Doran, 1942), p. 195.

[8] Lardner, op. cit., p. 28.

[9] Ottley, op. cit., p. 206.

[10] Ibid.

[11] Allison Danzig and Peter Brandwein, eds., The Greatest Sports Stories From The New York Times (New York: A. S. Barnes, 1951), pp. 77-80.

[12] Ottley, op. cit., p. 206.

[13] James P. Dawson, "Boxing," in Allison Danzig and Peter Brandwein, eds., Sport's Golden Age (New York: A. S. Barnes, 1948), p. 45.

[14] Congressional Record, 62nd Congress, 2nd session, 48:8 (July 1, 1912), 7890.

[15] Ibid., (July 1, 1912), 8551.

[16] Ibid., (July 10, 1912), 9305.

[17] Loc. cit.

[18] Loc. cit.

[19] Ibid., (August 1, 1912), 9988.

[20] Lardner, op.cit., pp. 31-32.

[21] Rose, op.cit., p. 131.

[22] Ottley, op.cit., p. 220.

[23] Ibid., p. 219.

[24] Ibid., p. 225.

[25] Lardner, op.cit., pp. 34-35.

[26] Ibid., p. 52.

[27] Ibid., pp. 50-51.

[28] Ibid., p. 56.

[29] New York Times, March 1, 1920, p. 23.

[30] Ibid., September 5, 1922, p. 17.

[31] Jonathan Mitchell, "Joe Louis Never Smiles," New Republic, 84 (October 9, 1935), 239.

[32] Lardner, op.cit., p. 40.

[33] Ottley, op.cit., p. 204.

[34]Ibid., p. 205.

[35]Robert Smith, Baseball (New York: Simon and Schuster, 1947), p. 315.

[36]Hy Turken and S. C. Thompson, The Official Encyclopedia of Baseball (New York: A. S. Barnes, 1951), p. 326.

[37]Lee Allen, 100 Years of Baseball (New York: Bartholomew House, 1950), pp. 281-282.

[38]Ibid., p. 282.

[39]Smith, op.cit., p. 318.

[40]Loc. cit.

[41]Allen, op.cit., p. 282.

[42]Loc. cit.

[43]Smith, op.cit., p. 320.

[44]Allen, op.cit., 282.

[45]Smith, op.cit., p. 323.

[46]Ottley, op.cit., p. 204.

[47]Oscar T. Barck, Jr., and Nelson M. Blake, Since 1900 (New York: MacMillan, 1952), p. 836.

[48]Loc. cit.

[49]Loc. cit.

[50]Loc. cit.

[51]New York Times, May 17, 1939, p. 12.

[52] Ibid., January 23, 1940, p. 7.

[53] Ibid., July 29, 1942, p. 23.

[54] Ibid., September 2, 1942, p. 14.

[55] Ibid., July 30, 1942, p. 14.

[56] Ibid., August 4, 1942, p. 18.

[57] Ibid., December 1, 1943, p. 22.

[58] Ibid., May 2, 1945, p. 28.

[59] Arthur Mann, "The Truth About the Jackie Robinson Case," Saturday Evening Post, 223 (May 13, 1950), 122.

[60] William Roeder, Jackie Robinson (New York: A. S. Barnes, 1949), p. 11 ff.

[61] Ibid., pp. 72-73.

[62] New York Times, April 25, 1945, p. 28.

[63] Ibid., May 4, 1945, p. 15.

[64] Ibid., April 19, 1945, p. 3.

[65] Ibid., April 23, 1945, p. 7.

[66] Mann, op. cit., p. 20.

[67] Roeder, op. cit., pp. 44-45.

[68] Ibid., p. 82.

[69] New York Times, October 24, 1945, p. 17.

[70] Loc. cit.

[71] Smith, op. cit., pp. 331.

[71a] Mann, op. cit., p. 123.

[72] Robert Smith, Baseball (New York: Simon and Schuster, 1947), p. 330.

[73] Ibid, p. 329.

[74] Loc. cit.

[75] Ibid., p. 330.

[76] New York Times, October 28, 1946, p. 23.

[77] Ibid., October 23, 1947, p. 38.

[78] Mann, op. cit., p. 123.

[79] Loc. cit.

[80] New York Times, February 18, 1948, p. 37.

[81] Ibid., February 19, 1948, p. 31.

[82] Mann, op. cit., p. 152.

[83] Ibid., p. 153.

[84] Lee Allen, 100 Years in Baseball (New York: Bartholomew House, 1950), pp. 287-288.

[85] Loc, cit.

[86] "You've Gotta be Crazy to Hate Jackie Robinson," New Review, 1 (September, 1954), 59-61.

[87]Ibid., p. 61.

[88]Ibid., p. 63.

[89]New York Times, July 4, 1947, p. 16.

[90]John Lardner, "The 50 Per Cent Color Line," Newsweek, 64, (May 10, 1954), 95.

[91]Frank G. Menke, The New Encyclopedia of Sports, (New York: A. S. Barnes, 1947), p. 741.

[92]Howard Cohn, "The Gibson Story," American Lawn Tennis, 34 (July, 1950), 7.

[93]Alice Marble, "A Vital Issue," American Lawn Tennis, 34 (July, 1950), 14.

[94]Loc. cit.

[95]Loc. cit.

[96]Walter White, "Time for a Progress Report," Saturday Review, 34 (September 22, 1951), p.39.

[97]New York Times, May 31, 1951, p.33.

[98]Gertye West Brown, "The Might Mite," Our Sports, 1 (May 1953), 36-39.

[99]Fresno Bee, July 7, 1957, p. 2S.

[100]New York Times, December 19, 1946, p. 5.

[101]Frederick Cozens and Florence Stumpf, Sports in American Life (Chicago: University of Chicago, 1953), p. 255.

[102]New York Times, July 23, 1949, p. 15.

[103]Ibid., October 17, 1949, p. 28.

[104] New York Times, January 28, 1950, p. 24.

[105] Cozens and Stumpf, op. cit., p. 256.

[106] New York Times, December 1, 1949, p. 47.

[107] Ibid., December 9, 1949, p. 40.

[108] Ibid., August 20, 1950, p. 37.

[109] Ibid., March 6, 1948, p. 17.

[110] Fresno Bee, January 15, 1952, p. 4B.

[111] Loc. cit.

[112] New York Times, January 20, 1952, p. 37.

CHAPTER II

THE CONTINUING STRUGGLE

Although there is now no sport in the United States from which Negroes are barred on a nationwide basis, there remains much racial segregation on regional and local levels. While most of the segregation has been found in the southern part of the United States, it has not been restricted to that area. In the last ten years many individual instances on the local and regional level have helped to reveal a pattern of segregation practices, both where segregation persists, and where it is giving way to the concept of mixed competition among Negroes and whites.

College Football

In college football, Negroes have played on northern college teams for more than fifty years. William H. Lewis, a Negro playing for Harvard University, was named to Walter Camp's All-American team in 1892 and 1893[1] and many Negroes since then have been similarly honored. However, before World War II northern college teams with Negroes on their rosters did not schedule games with southern colleges, or they left the Negro players at home when, if ever, they played against southern schools.

The years following World War II saw a change in the attitude of northern colleges. This was reflected when Nevada University cancelled a schedule game with Mississippi

State College in 1946 rather than leave a Negro player at home.[2] In the same year Pennsylvania State College cancelled a scheduled game with Miami University for the same reason.[3]

A change in attitude by at least one southern school also was shown when, in 1947, the University of Virginia permitted Chester Pierce, a Negro, of Harvard to stay in the University dormitory when Harvard played Virginia in Charlottesville, besides permitting him to play in the game. In the same year Pennsylvania State College cancelled a scheduled game with Miami University for the same reason.[3]

A change in attitude by at least one southern school also was shown when, in 1947, the University of Virginia permitted Chester Pierce, a Negro, of Harvard to stay in the University formitory when Harvard played Virginia in Charlottesville, besides permitting him to play in the game. In the same year Wilbur Williams, a Negro, played with a Staten Island professional football team in a game in Charlotte, North Caroline. He was the first Negro ever to play in a major white sporting event in that city. After the game he said, "I can say that I've never been treated more fairly and decently by an opposing team."[4]

Two Negroes, Wally Triplett and Dennis Hoggard, played for Penn State against Southern Methodist University in Dallas, Texas, in 1947, without incident.[5] In 1948 Oklahoma saw its first "mixed" football game[6] and in 1950 Negro players played against a white team in Florida for the first time in that state's history when the University of Iowa met the University of Miami in the Miami Orange Bowl stadium.[7]

On the other hand, Lafayette College in 1948 turned down a bid to the El Paso, Texas, Sun Bowl game because of a ban on a Negro player.[8] Also in 1948 the Washington

County, Maryland, Board of Education forced Hagerstown Junior College to cancel a game with Shippenburg State Teachers College of Pennsylvania because of a Negro on the latter school's team.[9]

In 1954 the first mixed football game ever played in Tennessee occurred without incident when Fisk University played against Taylor University of Indiana in the city of Nashville.[10] On the other hand, Millsboro, Delaware, High School withdrew from a scheduled game with Dover High School in 1955 because of the presence of Negroes on the Dover High School team, and the action was upheld by the Millsboro School Board.[11]

The Sugar Bowl Controversy

In December, 1955, the question of mixed football competition flared up in connection with the New Orleans post-season Sugar Bowl game.

The two teams chosen to play in the Sugar Bowl Game were Georgia Tech and the University of Pittsburgh. When it was learned that the Pittsburgh team had a Negro full-back, Bobby Grier, a member of the Georgia Board of Regents, R. V. Harris, and eight other board members urged that Georgia Tech not play in the game.[12] Georgia Governor S. Marvin Griffin wired the board his opinion that Georgia teams should be barred from playing against teams using Negroes, but Georgia Tech's President Blake R. Van Leer said that the school would play Pittsburgh whether the Negro was in the lineup or not.[13] Pittsburgh's Acting Chancellor Charles Nutting said the school would use Grier and permit him to live with the team in New Orleans.[14] Georgia Tech students staged a demonstration against Governor Griffin, and hanged him in effigy.[15]

The Board of Regents then voted 14 to 1 to permit the team to play, but adopted a resolution barring Georgia teams from any future post-season games in the South if segregation was not observed.[16]

The Sugar Bowl Game was played on January 2, 1956, in New Orleans with the Negro, Grier, in the Pittsburgh lineup. Some sports writers covering the game felt that a pass interference penalty called against Grier was unfair, but game officiels denied any racial bias behind the penalty. Otherwise the game was without incident.[17]

The Junior Rose Bowl

The 1955 Junior Rose Bowl Game in Pasadena caused controversy when Jones Junior College of Mississippi accepted an invitation to play against Compton College of California. On learning that Compton had several Negroes in its lineup, several Mississippi legislators tried to prevent Jones Junior College from playing the game.[18] They were unsuccessful, but after the game had been played, a bill was introduced into the Mississippi legislature barring college teams in the state from future games against teams using Negroes.[19]

Legislative Action in Louisiana

The 1956 Sugar Bowl incident started a series of legislative maneuvers in the state of Louisiana to prevent further racially mixed sports contests.

Three years previously, a bill introduced into the Louisiana legislature by State Senator B. H. Rogers of Grand Cane, which would have prohibited white men and Negroes from competing together in sports where admission was charged, had been soundly defeated.[20] In January, 1953, the Louisiana State Athletic Commission rescinded a sixty-year-old rule prohibiting Negro and white prize fighters from appearing on the same boxing program.[21]

In April, 1956, the Louisiana State University Board of Supervisors refused to act on a move made by board member J. Stewart Slack of Shreveport, executive of the White Citizens Councils Association of Louisiana, to ban mixed athletic events for Louisiana State teams at home or away. Slack promised to bring his motion up again at the next meeting of the board. [22]

At the next meeting of the board, slack's motion was voted on, and the supervisors' vote was in favor of letting Louisiana State athletes participate in mixed athletic events, on or off campus. [23]

Another college in the same state, however, took an opposite action, as Louisiana Tech officials withdrew from negotiations for a football game with the United States Air Force Academy because the Academy would not guarantee to field an all white team. [24]

Further racial problems in sports competition in the state of Louisiana were created by the presence of Negroes on two teams in the Evangeline League, a minor baseball league in Louisiana and Texas. On April 4, 1956, Niles David, the Recreation Commissioner of East Baton Rouge Parish, said visiting Evangeline League teams would not be allowed to use Negro players in the Baton Rouge City-owned baseball park. [25] Soon after this, David's ruling caused postponement of a scheduled game between Baton Rouge and Lake Charles, Louisiana, a team with two Negro players. [26] The league president, Ray Mullins, then awarded the game to Lake Charles by forfeit. [27]

The situation was resolved a week later when Lake Charles and Lafayette, Louisiana, the two teams with Negro players, agreed to transfer the five Negroes to another league. [28]

Louisiana's problems with racial segregation in sports resulted in the approval in

July, 1956, by the Louisiana legislature of a bill banning all further mixed athletic competition in the state.[29] Protests were heard from many sources, including the Mid-Winter Sports Association, promoters of the Sugar Bowl athletic events, and president Pierce Butler of the Texas Baseball League; and Louisiana Governor Earl Long was asked to veto the bill.[30] Long asked for expressions of opinions by the public and having received them, signed the bill. The governor reported that the majority of opinions he received favored the bill. He expected the bill to be given a court test, and while he said it had bad features, he criticized its opponents for their slowness in fighting it.[31]

The bill had several immediate results. Pittsburgh University barred acceptance of any further bids to the Sugar Bowl game; St. Louis University, Notre Dame, and Dayton University withdrew from the Sugar Bowl basketball tournament; and a basketball game scheduled between Marquette University of Milwaukee and Loyola University of New Orleans was cancelled.[32] Wisconsin University officials unofficially stated that the bill would probably result in cancellation of a football series between Wisconsin and Louisiana State.[33]

In September the Louisiana House of Representatives voted 67 to 15 to table the Tessier Bill which would have permitted mixed racial athletics in cities over 300,000. The bill, obviously aimed at maintaining the Sugar Bowl sports program, would have provided for segregated seating in stadiums and auditoriums except for specific blocks of seats sold outside Louisiana by visiting teams to Bowl events.[34]

The Louisiana bill prohibiting mixed athletic events ended a program which had been begun by Loyola University of New Orleans in 1954, when that school ended segregation among players and audiences at its basketball games.[35] Loyola had played against several teams with Negroes in the 1954-55 and 1955-56 basketball seasons, both in their opponents' gymnasiums and in their own gymnasium in New Orleans, with only one unfortunate incident. In 1956 while Loyola was playing Bradley University, one of the Bradley players, a Negro, became incensed at a decision of the referee and used profane language and vulgar gestures toward the officials, the other team, and the spectators. [36] This incident attracted nationwide attention, but three days later Loyola played the University of San Francisco, with four Negroes on its team, in the same gymnasium and San Francisco athletic director Phil Woopert reported afterward, "The crowd behaviour was completely enthusiastic and unbiased and the relationship between the players on both teams was completely exemplary."[37]

Policy Action in Mississippi

In Mississippi an unwritten but ironclad segregation policy adopted by all state institutions was revealed in December, 1956, when Mississippi State College withdrew from the Evansville, Indiana, College Invitational Basketball championship tournament rather than play against a team with a Negro in its starting lineup.[38]

On the following day the University of Mississippi withdrew from a tournament in Owensboro, Kentucky, rather than play against Iona College of New York, a team with Negro members. The United Press report of the action said:

> Strict bans on playing racially integrated teams grew out of a controversy over the appearance of Jones Junior College in the Junior Rose Bowl in Pasadena, California, in December, 1955. Several legislators had threatened to cut off Jones appropriation for playing Compton, California, College, a team with eight Negro Players.

> But the step was averted and several pro segregation bills died when the presidents of the state's 13 junior colleges agreed not to enter racially integrated contests. The policy was accepted as applying to all Mississippi

institutions.

The unwritten law this year prevented the appearance of two Mississippi junior colleges in national bowls. Both undefeated Pearl River and once beaten Jones were prime candidates for bids to post season bowls in Los Angeles and Pasadena.[39]

Baseball in the South

In baseball, a variety of incidents since the major color line was broken in 1946 have shown both a gradual acceptance of the idea of integration in some parts of the South and a stubborn resistance to it in others.

In 1952 the Dallas team in the Texas League signed a Negro pitcher, Dave Hoskins, amid predictions that this action would cause trouble in all the cities in the league. However, by the middle of the 1952 season the Fresno Bee felt justified in commenting editorially:

> But since he was signed, no riots have occurred and the only disturbance in evidence has been the increased clicking of the turnstiles when Hoskins pitches and the loud cheers from the fans in the grandstand.

> So ancient prejudices do yield to the march of time, and the principle that a human being should be judged on the basis of his performances, not on the color of his skin, wins ever wider acceptance.[40]

In the following season the Hot Springs, Arkansas, team in the Cotton States League signed a Negro pitcher, George Turgeson. Upon protests from other teams in the league, he was optioned to another league.[41] Later in the season the Hot Springs management called Turgeson back. When he was scheduled to appear against Jackson, Mississippi, on May 20, the Jackson players refused to take the field.[42] League officials ruled the game forfeited to Jackson, on the grounds that Hot Springs had no right to ask the Jackson players to play against a Negro.[43]

-38-

This action was overruled a month later by George Trautman, the commissioner of minor league baseball, who said that league president Al Haraway's action in forfeiting the game to Jackson was illegal. He further ruled that any action by the league to prevent the use of Negro players was also illegal, adding that in such actions the league "is at war with the concept that the national pastime offers equal opportunity to all."[44]

The following year Hot Springs again signed a Negro player, and this time when they inserted him into the lineup against Meridian, Mississippi, on July 20, nothing unusual happend. A witness said that the Negro appeared to be well received.[45]

In 1955 the Pine Bluff, Arkansas, team in the same Cotton States League signed three Negro players early in the season,[46] only to drop them three days later, blaming pressure brought to bear by the other teams in the league.[47]

The city of Birmingham, Alabama, on March 22, 1954, amended a segregation law which said, in part, "It shall be unlawful for a Negro and a white person to play together, or in company with each other, in any games of cards, dice, dominoes, checkers, baseball, softball, football, basketball, or similar games." The amended law permitted professional football and baseball exhibitions with mixed teams. Several major league baseball teams using Negroes played exhibition games there during the spring, but die-hard white supremacists circulated petitions arguing that mixed baseball would lead to "mongrelization." Early in June, Birmingham's citizens voted overwhelmingly to restore segregation to sports.[48]

The ban on mixed athletic competition in Birmingham caused cancellation of a scheduled exhibition baseball game between Brooklyn and Milwaukee in that city in April, 1956[49] and also cancellation of two exhibition games between Pittsburgh and Kansas City in Birmingham.[50] A scheduled game between Cleveland and New York in Meridian, Mississippi, was cancelled also because of segregation rulings.[51]

Antipathy to mixed baseball competition in some parts of the South extended down to the childhood level. In 1955 a Negro Little League baseball team entered the South Carolina state championship tournament, and 53 white teams withdrew in protest. The Negro team was awarded the championship by default, but was barred from advancing to the regional tournament.[52]

In the same year in a community in Florida, five white Little League teams refused to play the one Negro team in the tournament. National Headquarters of Little League Baseball disqualified the five white teams from tournament play and advanced the Negro team to the next tournament level.[53]

According to Creighton J. Hale, Director of Research for Little League Baseball, "In 1956, no situations developed as was true of 1955. We realize that his is a very controversial problem, but we will always stand firm on our policy of no racial discrimination."[54]

Other Incidents

Several other incidents indicate a relaxing of barriers against mixed sports competition in other parts of the South. On December 22, 1951, the first mixed boxing match in the history of the state of Florida took place between Kid Gavilan, a Negro from Cuba, and Bobby Dykes, white, of Miami, in Miami Stadium.[55] On November 27, 1951, Howard Richardson, a Negro jockey, received the first license to ride on Florida tracks ever granted to a Negro.[56]

In 1954 a Texas Appeals Court held unconstitutional a law banning mixed prize fights in that state.[57] The Texas Supreme Court refused to reverse this ruling,[58] and

on February 24, 1955, the first mixed boxing match in Texas history was held. I. H.

Harvey, a Negro, lost a unanimous decision to Buddy Turman, white, of Tyler, Texas.

The crowd of 2,400 was the largest to watch a fight in Dallas in more than a decade.

Frank Biehl, the house manager, said about 1,000 of the fans were Negroes.[59]

Malcolm Whitfield, a Negro track star, was the first member of his race to re-

ceive the James E. Sullivan Memorial Trophy as the outstanding United States amateur

athlete. The award is presented annually by the National Amateur Athletic Union to "the

amateur athlete who, by performance, example and good influence, did most to advance

the cause of good sportsmanship during the year." In 1954 Whitfield was the first choice

on 252 of the 657 ballots cast by sports writers all over the nation.[60]

The use of two Negroes in an Oak Ridge, Tennessee, High School basketball game

marked the first break in segregation in a Tennessee school athletic event.[61]

In the spring of 1956, George Harris, a Negro, tried out for the University of

Virginia football team. He was the first Negro ever to do so at the University. Later

Harris was forced to drop from the team because of academic difficulties, but he stated

he would remain at the University rather than transfer to a Negro college. "I like the

school, I like the fellows, and I like the faculty," he said.[62]

An indication of an end to segregation in another area of the country might also be

noted. In 1954 a Negro team was permitted to enter the amateur East End Baseball

League in Suffolk, New York. It was the first time a Negro team had been allowed in the

League.[63]

Footnotes

[1] Frederick Cozens and Florence Stumpf, Sports in American Life (Chicago: University of Chicago, 1953), p. 251.

[2] Fresno Bee, November 4, 1946, p. 12.

[3] New York Times, November 6, 1946, p. 33.

[4] Ibid., October 14, 1947, p. 34.

[5] Cozens and Stumpf, op.cit, p. 252.

[6] New York Times, October 24, 1948, p. V6.

[7] Cozens and Stumpf, loc. cit.

[8] New York Times, November 24, 1948, p. 27.

[9] Ibid., February 18, 1948, p. 37.

[10] Ibid, October 28, 1954, p. 20.

[11] Ibid., December 1, 1955, p. 48.

[12] Ibid.

[13] Ibid., December 3, 1945, p. 1

[14] Loc. cit.

[15] Ibid., December 4, 1955, p. 1.

[16] Ibid., December 6, 1955, p. 1.

[17] Ibid., January 3, 1956, p. 23.

[18] New York Times, December 6, 1955, p. 32.

[19] Ibid., January 19, 1956, p. 22.

[20] Ibid., June 4, 1952, p. 19.

[21] Ibid., January 24, 1953, p. 37.

[22] Fresno Bee, April 8, 1956, p. 58.

[23] New York Times, May 29, 1956, p. 56.

[24] Ibid., March 17, 1956, p. 1.

[25] Ibid., April 5, 1956, p. 22.

[26] Ibid., April 29, 1956, p. 48.

[27] Fresno Bee, May 1, 1956, p. 6B.

[28] New York Times, May 7, 1956, p. 17.

[29] Ibid., July 13, 1956, p. 20.

[30] Ibid., July 15, 1956, p. 51.

[31] Ibid, July 17, 1956, p. 13.

[32] Ibid., July 29, 1956, p. 4.

[33] Ibid., July 20, 1956, p. 19.

[34] Ibid., September 1, 1956, p. 6.

[35] Ibid., November 26, 1954, p. 18.

[36] Fresno Bee, December 21, 1955, p. 7B.

[37] Letter from Mr. Woolpert to the writer, September 19, 1956.

[38] Fresno Bee, December 30, 1956, p. 1S.

[39] Ibid., December 31, 1956, p. 3B.

[40] Ibid., July 8, 1952, p. 18B.

[41] New York Times, April 21, 1953, p. 36.

[42] Ibid., May 21, 1953, p. 28.

[43] Ibid., May 22, 1953, p. 33.

[44] Ibid., June 7, 1953, p. 32.

[45] Fresno Bee, July 21, 1954, p. 7B.

[46] New York Times, May 5, 1955, p. 44.

[47] Ibid., May 8, 1955, p. V3.

[48] "The National Game," Time, LXIII (June 14, 1954), p. 46.

[49] New York Times, February 15, 1956, p. 26.

[50] Ibid., February 16, 1956, p. 20.

[51] Ibid., March 3, 1956, p. 10.

[52] Ibid., July 25, 1955, p. 25.

[53] Letter to the writer from Creighton J. Hale, January 10, 1957.

[54] Loc. cit.

[55] New York Times, December 23, 1951, p. 40.

[56] Ibid., November 28, 1951, p. 33.

[57] Ibid., October 28, 1954, p. 20.

[58] Ibid., January 20, 1955, p. 35.

[59] Fresno Bee, February 25, 1955, p. 3B.

[60] Ibid., December 31, 1954, p. 4B.

[61] New York Times, December 4, 1955, p. 62.

[62] Fresno Bee, February 29, 1956, p. 7B.

[63] New York Times, May 19, 1954, p. 22.

CHAPTER III

THE PRESENT SITUATION

It is difficult accurately to assess the present extent of discrimination against the

Negro in American athletic competition for two reasons. One is that the situation is a

fluid one, with frequent changes occurring in segregation policies of areas or groups.

The other is that much of the discrimination that still exists is of the tacit "gentlemen's

agreement" or "unwritten law" type about which little direct information can be obtained.

However, some definite information is available which gives some indication of

the pattern of sports segregation still existing in this country.

For the purposes of this paper, letters were sent to the secretaries of state of

fourteen states in the southern part of the United States requesting information as to

whether or not the state had any legislation governing mixed athletic competition among

Negroes and whites. The states contacted were Texas, Oklahoma, Arkansas, Mississippi,

Alabama, Louisiana, Florida, Georgia, South Caroline, North Carolina, Virginia, West

Virginia, Tennessee, and Maryland.[1]

In addition, letters were sent to twenty colleges in the southern part of the United

States which have athletic programs ambitious enough to include intersectional competi-

tion. The directors of athletics at these colleges were asked if their schools had any

policy, written or unwritten, in regard to scheduling games with teams which might have negro players. As an item of additional information, the athletic directors were asked whether, in their opinions, there has been a tendency toward more or less restriction of mixed athletic competition in recent years.

The institutions so contacted were the University of Texas, Southern Methodist University in Texas, the University of Miami, Auburn University, Vanderbilt University in Tennessee, Duke University in North Carolina, Oklahoma City University, and the state universities of Oklahoma, Arkansas, Mississippi, Alabama, Louisiana, Florida, Georgia, South Carolina, North Carolina, Virginia, West Virginia, Tennessee, and Maryland.[2]

Letters were sent to twenty other colleges in other sections of the country. These inquired of the directors of athletics whether the colleges had any policy, written or unwritten, in regard to the scheduling of games with teams which had prohibitions against competition with negro athletes, or in areas where mixed racial competition is prohibited. These athletic directors also were asked whether in their opinions there has been any increase or decrease in racial segregation in sports in recent years.

The institutions contacted were The University of California at Los Angeles, the University of San Francisco, the University of Washington, the University of Nebraska, Pittsburgh University, Ohio State University, Yale University, the University of Pennsylvania, Michigan State University, the University of Wisconsin, Montana State College, Columbia University, the University of Notre Dame, the University of Iowa, Marquette University in Wisconsin, San Jose State College, the University of Colorado, the University of Illinois, Northwestern University in Illinois, and Drake University in Iowa.[3]

While many of the persons or institutions contacted did not reply, others proved very helpful and supplied much information. In addition, newspaper accounts in recent years have reported some institutions adopting definite policies in regard to racial segregation in athletics. Incidents of record have also served to indicate a policy or lack of policy in certain areas.

Of the six secretaries of state for the states in the South who replied to the request for information, only one stated that there was an actual state law which prohibited athletic competition between Negroes and white men. This was the state of Louisiana, whose passage of such a law has already been noted.[4] The secretary enclosed a copy of the Louisiana law, which is included with this paper.[5]

The Eugene Cook Attorney General for the state of Georgia, forwarded a copy of a compilation of Georgia laws relating to segregation of the races which revealed that in the 1955 session of the Georgia legislature, HB #555 which would prohibit mixed athletic events and dances and provide penalties for violations thereof did not pass.[6] In the 1956 session, HB #18, prohibiting mixed athletic events and dances and declaring it a misdemeanor to hold or direct same or participate in such game or event, was postponed indefinitely in the House on February 12, 1956.[7]

Miss Alta C. Patton, Legislative Analyst for the state of Alabama, wrote:

> Alabama has no law of statewide application requiring segregation of the races at athletic contests or forbidding joint participation of any and all races in such sports as baseball, football, basketball, or boxing.

> However, many municipalities in the State have adopted ordinances forbidding athletic contests in which participants are of both the white and negro races. And some municipalities require the segregation of the races in the audience at all public entertainments, including athletic contests.[8]

Replies from the states of Florida and North Carolina reported merely that the states had no such laws. The secretary of state for the state of Texas stated that his office did not have the physical facilities for research of this type. However, it is a matter of public record that in 1954 a Texas Appeals Court held unconstitutional a law banning mixed prize fights in that state,[9] and that mixed athletic competition has taken place in football and baseball in Texas within the last three years without legal repercussions.[10]

Mixed athletic competition has also taken place in the states of Oklahoma, Tennessee, Maryland, Virginia, West Virginia within the last three years without legal action, indicating either an absence of state laws forbidding such competition or a policy of non-enforcement.

Three of the athletic directors of southern colleges replied to the inquiry. Of these, two reported a definite policy on non-discrimination, while one reported his school had no written policy but had never played against teams with Negro players.

Lester Jordan, Business Manager of Athletics at Southern Methodist University in Dallas, Texas, wrote:

> SMU has never been unwilling to play teams with Negro players either at home or away. One of the first teams in the southwest to play against Negroes away from home was the SMU football team of 1935. You may recall that SMU also was the first team to play a team with Negro players in the Cotton Bowl. This was on Junuary 1, 1948 when Penn State was the opponent. Matty Bell, Athletic Director at SMU and former football coach, has been a leader in breaking down racial barriers in athletics.[11]

Dana X. Bible, Director of Athletics at the University of Texas, wrote: "The University of Texas athletic teams participate against teams that have Negro players in games on our home field and away."[12]

Percy Beard, General Manager of the University of Florida Division of Intercollegiate Athletics, wrote:

> I do not know of any written policy regarding this question. To the best of my knowledge we have never played any team which had Negro players

either at home or away. If any teams had Negro players they did not play against us.[13]

Mr. Beard also gave his opinion that the Supreme Court's ruling on school integration has stiffened opposition in the South to all forms of racial integration -- athletic and otherwise.[14]

Although they did not reply to the inquiry, officials of Mississippi State College and the University of Mississippi have indicated a policy not to compete athletically against schools with Negro players, a policy which applies to the state's other colleges and junior colleges as well.[15]

Action by the Georgia Board of Regents applies a bar to that state's universities also from athletic competition in which segregation is not observed.[16]

On the other hand, the University of Virginia has indicated a policy of non-segregation in allowing Negro player to try out for the university's own football team.[17]

Along the same lines, Oklahoma City University, which in 1946 refused to play Fresno State College in football if Fresno State used Negro players,[18] in 1957 reported having two Negroes on its baseball team.[19]

Of the seven institutions outside of the South whose athletic directors replied to the inquiry, all seven reported either definite policies against scheduling games with teams in areas where segregation is practiced, unwritten policies not to schedule games in these areas, of the definition conviction that the school never would schedule a game in which racial discrimination would be practiced.

Those making a definite statement of policy included Wilbur C. Johns, Director of Athletics at the University of California at Los Angeles, who said: "We have a definite policy of not scheduling in areas where all athletes are not given exactly the same privileges. This means housing, feeding, transportation, and competition."[20]

George Briggs, Director of Athletics at the University of Washington, said: "The University of Washington does not schedule athletic contests with schools either in Seattle or in their home area where participation of Negro athletes is prohibited or discouraged." He added that the University of Washington recently concluded a home-and-home series with Baylor University of Waco, Texas and that the experience was most favorable, both in Seattle and in Texas. There was no problem of Negro participation, and the university had several on its squad at the time.[21]

Richard C. Larkins, Director of Athletics at The Ohio State University, wrote: We do not schedule schools regardless of the area who object to playing against our Negro athletes."[22]

DeLaney Kiphuth, Director of Athletics at Yale University, wrote: "Our only policy is to avoid the scheduling of teams with any policy of racial discrimination." He added that a thorough check of all sources revealed no feeling against Negroes on the Yale basketball team at the Orange Bowl basketball tournament in Miami.[23]

Jeremiah Ford II, Director of Athletics at the University of Pennsylvania, stated: "The University of Pennsylvania has no policy, official or unofficial, in regard to scheduling of athletic contests with schools in areas where segregation is practiced or where participation of Negro athletes is prohibited or discouraged." However, he then added, "The University of Pennsylvania teams travel, eat, sleep, and participate as a unit. We do not practice segregation here and will permit no opponent segregation against any members of our teams or staff."[24]

While reporting that the University of San Francisco has no official policy in regard to scheduling games in areas where segregation is practiced, Phil Woolpert, athletic director of the university, added: "I feel justified in saying, however, unofficially but very positively, that I am certain our Administration would not agree to the participation of any of our athletic teams in a state such as Louisiana which practices this type of prohibition. In fact, I am positive that we would boycott any area which practices discrimination regardless of whether or not we have Negro athletes on our team."[25]

The letter to the University of Nebraska inquiring as to the University's policies was returned unsigned with the handwritten note "We use them (Negro athletes) and have no trouble."

In addition to those institutions replying to the letter of inquiry, several others have indicated by their actions or by public statements that they will not permit their teams to compete in areas where Negro members of the teams might be discriminated against.

The athletic board of the University of Indiana announced publicly in the spring of 1956 that they would refuse to schedule games from which Negro players were barred. Public approval of this policy was expressed by representatives of Purdue University, the University of Notre Dame, and Butler University.[26]

Athletic officials at the United States Air Force Academy in Colorado also indicated such a policy when they refused to guarantee an all white team for a proposed football game with Louisiana Tech in 1956.[27]

Similar action has been taken in the past by the University of Wisconsin, which withdrew from a scheduled track meet at Columbia, Missouri, in 1939 when it was learned that a Negro hurdler, Ed Smith, would not be allowed to compete.[28]

In 1946 the University of Nevada cancelled a scheduled football game with Mississippi State College rather than leave a Negro player at home,[29] and in the same year Pennsylvania State College withdrew from a scheduled game with Miami University for the same reason.[30] In 1948 Lafayette College turned down a bid to the El Paso, Texas, Sun Bowl football game because of a ban on a Negro player.[31]

In the realm of baseball, a report published early in 1957 indicated that only one of the 16 teams in the two major leagues had no Negro players on its roster.

This was the Washington, D. C., team of the American League. However, club officials denied that there was any racial discrimination involved, or that any deliberate policy of not using Negro players was being followed.[32]

The same officials, who also control the Washington, D. C., team in the National Professional Football League, denied in the same statement any policy of racial discrimination on the Washington Redskins professional football team. The Washington team is the only one in the league which used no Negro players in the 1956 season.[33]

Footnotes

[1]See Appendix A.

[2]See Appendix B.

[3]See Appendix C.

[4]Cf. p. 45.

[5]See Appendix D.

[6] Compilation of Georgia Laws and Opinions of the Attorney General relating to Segregation of the Races, Eugene Cook, ed., (Atlanta: State of Georgia, 1956), p. 89.

[7] Ibid., p. 90.

[8] Letter from Miss Alta C. Patton, August 16, 1956

[9] Cf. pp. 52-53.

[10] Cf. pp. 39, 48.

[11] Letter from Mr. Jordan, November 15, 1956.

[12] Letter from Mr. Bible, November 5, 1956.

[13] Letter from Mr. Beard, November 4, 1956.

[14] Loc. cit.

[15] Cf. p. 46.

[16] Cf. p. 41.

[17] Cf. p. 52.

[18] Fresno Bee, October 14, 1956, p. 12.

[19] Ibid., March 5, 1957, p. 26.

[20] Letter from Mr. Johns, September 13, 1956.

[21] Letter from Mr. Briggs, September 5, 1956.

[22] Letter from Mr. Larkins, August 27, 1956.

[23] Letter from Mr. Kiphuth, September 4, 1956.

[24] Letter from Mr. Ford, August 30, 1956.

[25] Letter from Mr. Woolpert, September 19, 1956.

[26] New York Times, March 24, 1956, p. 15.

[27] Ibid., March 17, 1956, p. 1.

[28] Ibid., April 5, 1939, p. 34.

[29] Fresno Bee, November 4, 1946, p. 12.

[30] New York Times, November 6, 1946, p. 33.

[31] Ibid., November 24, 1948, p. 27.

[32] Fresno Bee, February 12, 1957, p. 5B.

[33] Loc. cit.

CHAPTER IV

CONCLUSIONS

However inconclusive the available evidence on the present extent of discrimination against Negroes in American athletic activities may be, one obvious fact can be stated with assurance. There is far less discrimination in American athletic activities in 1957 than there was as recently as 1945.

In 1945 there were no Negroes in organized baseball, nor had there been since 1890. No Negro had ever played in a major American tennis tournament, in a major national golf tournament, or in the national bowling championship tournament. Since 1945, participation of Negroes in all of these events has become commonplace.

Whether this trend will continue and there will be increasingly wider participation by Negroes in American sports activities, or whether such actions as that of the Louisiana legislature in banning mixed athletic events will be emulated in other areas and prove a deterrent to further racial desegregation in sports remains to be seen. However, the opinions of a number of individuals who have had close personal contact with the sports world in various ways are worth noting.

Jesse Owens, Negro track star of the 1936 Olympic Games in Berlin, who was recently sponsored by the State Department on a tour of Asia, Africa, and Europe to speak on his experiences as an athlete and to demonstrate proper athletic techniques, said on his return:

> I believe that this trip showed that sports are one of the best ways to help
> bring about international understanding and also understanding among the races.
> I know I am convinced that as long as people can compete together peacefully in
> games and sports, we will have a pretty good chance for a peaceful world. [1]

Althea Gibson, the first Negro ever to compete in the United States Lawn Tennis

Association national tournament at Forest Hills, New York, also had State Department

sponsorship in a tour of Europe in 1956, during which she played in most of the major

European tournaments. Shortly after her return to this country, Miss Gibson stated:

> It used to be that people assumed that my being a Negro was my greatest
> handicap to ever playing championship tennis. Now nobody considers that
> important. The things they worry about are my ground strokes, and whether
> my net game will ever be good enough for me to win the national championship. [2]

Will Connolly, columnist for the San Francisco Chronicle, wrote, shortly after the

Louisiana legislature had passed its ban on mixed athletic contests:

> The gentlemen in Louisiana can ban, for the time being, any further such
> contests in their own state, but they cannot legislate against history. The
> simple fact is that many thousands of people in the South have seen white men
> and Negroes play together on the same teams, with no dire or unhappy results.
> Millions more can see the same thing any week of the year on nationally televised
> sports events. In the face of this visual evidence, the idea that there is some
> threat to the white man's civilization in the presence of Negroes and whites on
> the same baseball diamond, the same tennis courts, or the same football field
> simply cannot survive, any more than the belief that a heavier object falls faster
> than a lighter one could survive Galileo's visual demonstration from the Tower
> of Pisa. [3]

Finally, Branch Rickey, the baseball executive who broke baseball's unwritten law

against the use of Negro players, has said:

> When I signed Robinson and the other Negroes to the Brooklyn team, I
> did not have the fond delusion that this would bring about an overnight change in
> our social attitudes. To me they were just good baseball players who were
> available and who could help our team. However, I believed then as I believe
> now that the world of sports offers one of our finest mediums for showing that
> a man should be judged by what he does, not by what his color is. I am con-

vinced that some day the Negro will take his place in American society un-
marked by any racial stigma or taint. I will not live to see it, but it will
come. And baseball will have done its part to help it come.[4]

An analysis of the information discussed in the preceding chapters of this paper

suggests two possible conclusions about the immediate future in regard to racial segrega-

tion in American sports.

One of these is that among northern colleges there is a growing resolve not to

schedule athletic contests with schools, or in areas where there might be discrimination

against Negro athletes. This was indicated by the replies of the seven athletic directors

who replied to the inquiry about their schools' policies, as well as by the actions of other

northern colleges which have been reported in the press.

This can have one of two possible effects on those southern colleges who still ob-

serve racial segregation and who expect their opponents to do so as well. Either they

will find it increasingly difficult to schedule intersectional games, which are usually very

lucrative from the standpoint of gate receipts, and will be confined to playing against

schools from their own region; or they will be forced eventually to modify their policies

in order to return the national prestige in athletics which they have enjoyed in the past.

A second conclusion which can be drawn is that while there has been a general

tendency toward lowering the bars against mixed sports competition in the South in recent

years, that tendency has been reversed during the last two or three years, at least in

such states as Louisiana, Mississippi, and Georgia.

It seems reasonable to believe that this recent reversal is part of a general reac-

tion in the South against the historic Supreme Court decision of May 17, 1954, ruling

segregation in public schools to be unconstitutional. Rather than conform with this decision, many southern leaders have attempted to strengthen such segregation barriers as already exist. In the state of Louisiana this has included the outlawing of all forms of mixed athletic competition. In Georgia and Mississippi it has meant prohibiting the colleges and junior colleges in those states from meeting teams with Negro players.

To those who look forward to an eventual peaceful settlement of all difficulties between the races, these reverses may prove discouraging. However, these idealists may take encouragement from certain demonstrable results which can be shown from improved racial relationships in the field of sports. One of these is an uplift in the morale of the Negro people as a whole when members of their race achieve eminence in various sports. Another is a general lessening of racial animosities among those white athletes who compete on the same teams with, or who compete against, Negro athletes.

The tendency of the Negro people to take pride in the achievements of members of their race, sometimes out of proportion to the actual importance of the achievements, has been noted by several sociologists. Arnold M. Rose pointed out this tendency, which was not always, he felt, a healthy one. Then he added:

> A much more healthy phenomenon for society was the contribution to the race pride of the Negro masses made by the pugilistic success of Joe Louis. Joe Louis had been born in Alabama and he worked in a Detroit factory; thus, unlike most of the other Negro successes, he was one of the lower class at the time of his victory in 1935. This fight was with Primo Carnera, an Italian, and the time was during the Italo-Ethiopian War, when Negro sympathies were strongly with the darker contender. When Louis won, Negroes celebrated publicly, at least in the North.
>
> . . . He gave the little fellow of the race the long-awaited chance to shout and yell - and indeed to brag and boast. But he also gave Negroes confidence which enabled them to meet with increased authority their day-to day problems . . . . The Pittsburgh Courier held that Louis "lifted an entire race out of the slough of inferiority, and gave them a sense of self-importance." There is perhaps a little yeast contained in that statement, but it is a fact that Joe gave a decided lift to the Negro's morale by stimu-

lating a more positive outlook on American Life.[5]

An example of the lessening of racial animosities among white athletes who compete on the same teams with, or who compete against, Negro athletes, can be found in the field of baseball.

When Branch Rickey brought Jackie Robinson into the major leagues in 1947, not only were there many who entertained personal doubts that the experiement would be successful, there were also at least three definite attempts by groups of players to prevent Robinson's playing. These were the proposed circulation of a petition among his own Brooklyn team mates asking that Robinson be kept off the team, the threat of the Philadelphia team not to take the field if Robinson played, and the proposed players strike projected by members of the St. Louis team.[6]

While all of these attempts were thwarted, they may certainly be construed to indicate that a number of players were hostile to Negroes as major league baseball players. However, after Robinson's success in the 1947 season acceptance of Negroes became common. In the nine baseball seasons that have gone by since that time, several hundred Negroes have entered organized baseball, without a single important incident.

A writer for Our Sports magazine in 1953 discussed the question "What White Big Leaguers Really Think of Negro Players." He reported talks with players and officials from all parts of the country. In answering the question, "Have Negroes really been accepted in organized baseball?" he wrote:

> A flip answer would be a wrong answer because it is not a flippant situation. This much is certain: baseball has advanced. It has traveled a long way down the road to brotherhood and a handful of bigots can no more stop the advances to come than they can turn back the ones accomplished. The bigots are being beaten and the most encouraging thing is that only a handful of them are left. . . .

There may be a few more bad moments before baseball's last racial incident is over. But for every moment of tension, there'll be a thousand hours when democracy is quietly in action.

Are there still bigots in baseball?

A few, but they're all hiding under their beds.[7]

Jackie Robinson himself had experienced the way in which racial feelings can be ameliorated when white and Negro athletes are members of the same team, even before he entered organized baseball. In 1940 he was a member of the college all-star football team, which also included several southern players. At first, he later reported, there was some slight coolness in the training camp, but this soon gave way, and all the players became friendly. "It proves, or at least indicates to me," he said, "that once the ice is broken and the idea accepted, the thing is entirely possible."[8]

The late Walter White, long-time secretary of the National Association for the Advancement of Colored People, was one Negro leader who was highly encouraged over the rapid and widespread acceptance of Negroes in baseball, although he was realistic enough to see that this acceptance had a strong profit motive behind it as well as a sense of justice. Shortly before his death, he wrote:

> The phenomenal success of Negroes in organized baseball is not entirely due to sentimentality or to an abstract sense of fair play. American baseball is as hardheaded a business operation as is General Motors. Owners and managers have learned to their delight that there are not only an abundant number of excellent Negro ball players, but that, because of them, attendance at games, not only by Negroes but also by other Americans, is measurably increased. Thus, excellent profits fortuitously combined with American precepts of fair play have created a major chance of racial mores, which has percolated even down to minor leagues in the Deep South.

> In 1945 any person who dared predict that colored professional baseball players would soon play on Southern teams would have been thought insane. By 1954 Negroes were playing professional ball on local teams in Florida, Oklahoma, Virginia, Louisiana, Texas, and Georgia. However, the Attorney

General of Mississippi ruled in 1953 that "it was against public policy" to permit two Negro players of Hot Springs, Arkansas, Class C Cotton States League to play against white players in Mississippi. The bitter quarrel that was thereby set off brought widespread disapproval of the Mississippi official's action. George M. Trautman, President of the Minor Leagues, bluntly declared: "Any provision by any league against the employment by a club of any individual, because of his race, color, or creed, cannot and will not be approved." Nevertheless, Mississippi was adamant, even when a Negro player of the Jacksonville, Florida, team was named Most Valuable Player of the Year in the Class A South Atlantic League.

The additional burdens and responsibilities of Negro professional baseball players, beyond those of their white team mates, are not yet over, as the Mississippi episode shows. But in 1954 there remained no doubt that the major obstackes had been overcome, as far as Negro players of talent were concerned, in the lucrative business of professional baseball.[9]

One more conclusion may be drawn from a study of race relations in organized sports. That is, where direct, positive action is taken to improve the lot of a minority group such as the Negroes, that action will generally have positive results. Just as such legislation as FEPC and the Ives-Quinn Act resulted in demonstrable gains for Negroes in employment opportunities, and as the use of law officers or militia to enforce school integration in certain parts of the South has succeeded in its immediate purpose, so direct action to enforce racial equality in sports competition has been successful.

Where player strikes threatened the entrance of Negroes into organized baseball, the direct, forceful action of Branch Rickey and Ford Drick quickly erased the threats. Where the introduction of resolutions to various legislative and quasi-legislative bodies, asking that baseball abandon discrimination, and the appointment of committees to study the problem, accomplished nothing,[10] Rickey accomplished an end to the baseball color line through the simple, direct act of signing a Negro baseball player to a contract -- literally, he accomplished it with the stroke of a pen.

There are many who contend that, "Human nature cannot be changed by legislation," and that the settlement of this nation's ancient, deep-seated racial problems will take much time and patience. Unquestionably this is true. But the Negro athlete is not interested in changing human nature. All he wants is an equal chance in competition -- a chance to win whatever fame, garner whatever laurels, reap whatever financial rewards his ability and determination entitle him to.

Many obstacles still confront him. Many problems remain to be solved. But today, in 1957, he has a better chance to reach these goals than he has ever had before.

Footnotes

[1] Visalia Times-Delta, November 6, 1956, p. 9.

[2] Los Angeles Times, August 5, 1956, p. 37.

[3] Will Connolly, San Francisco Chronicle, July 22, 1956, p. S1.

[4] Arthur Mann, "The Truth About the Jackie Robinson Case," Saturday Evening Post, 223 (May 13, 1950), 20.

[5] Arnold M. Rose, The Negro's Morale, Minneapolis: University of Minnesota Press, 1949), pp. 53-54.

[6] Cf. pp. 27-28.

[7] Roger Kahn, "What White Big Leaguers Really Think of Negroes," Our Sports, 1 (June, 1953), 64-65.

[8] John T. Winterich, "Playing Ball," Saturday Review, 28 November 24, 1945, 12.

[9] Walter White, How Far the Promised Land, (New York: Viking Press, 1956), p. 185.

[10] Cf. pp. 19-22.

BIBLIOGRAPHY

A. BOOKS

Allen, Lee. 100 Years of Baseball. New York: Bartholomew House, 1950. 314 pp.

Anonymous. Cavalcade of the American Negro. Chicago: Diamond Jubilee Exposition Authority, 1940. 95 pp.

Barck, Oscar P. Jr. and Nelson M. Blake. Since 1900. New York: Macmillan, 1952. 903 pp.

Butcher, Margaret. The Negro in American Culture. New York: Knopf, 1956. 294 pp.

Chidsey, Donald. John the Great. Garden City: Doubleday Doran, 1942. 337 pp.

Cozens, Frederick and Florence Stumpf. Sports in American Life. Chicago: University of Chicago, 1953. 366 pp.

Danzig, Allison and Peter Brandwein, editors. The Greatest Sports Stories From the New York Times. New York: A. S. Barnes, 1948. 358 pp.

Dawson, James P., "Boxing," in Allis Danzig and Peter Brandwein, editors, Sports Golden Age. New York: A. S. Barnes, 1951. 427 pp.

DuBois, William E. B. Dusk of Dawn. New York: Harcourt, Brace, 1940. 334 pp.

_____ The Souls of Black Folk. Chicago: A. C. McClurg, 1915. 264 pp.

Dulles, Foster Rhea. America Learns to Play. New York: D. Appleton-Century, 1940. 441 pp.

Henderson, Edwin Bancroft. The Negro in Sports. Washington, D. C.: Associated Publishers, 1949. 507 pp.

Johnson, Charles S. The Negro in American Civilization. New York: Henry Holt, 1930. 538 pp.

Lardner, John. White Hopes and Other Tigers. Philadelphia: J. B. Lippincott, 1947. 185 pp.

Louis, Joe and others. My Life Story. New York: Duell, Sloan and Pearce, 1947. 188 pp.

Menke, Frank G. The New Encyclopedia of Sports. New York: A. S. Barnes, 1947. 1007 pp.

Myrdal, Gunnar. An American Dilemma. New York: Harper, 1944. 1483 pp.

Ottley, Roi. Black Odyssey. New York: Scribner's, 1950. 248 pp.

_____ New World A'Coming. Boston: Houghton Mifflin, 1943. 227 pp.

Quillin, Frank U. The Color Line in Ohio. Ann Arbor: G. Wahr, 1913. 178 pp.

Robinson, John R. and Wendell Smith. Jackie Robinson. New York: A. S. Barnes, 1948. 183 pp.

Rose, Arnold M. The Negro's Morale. Minneapolis: University of Minnesota, 1945. 153 pp.

_____ The Negro in America. New york: Harper, 1948. 325 pp.

Smith, Robert. Baseball. New York: Simon and Schuster, 1947. 362 pp.

Tunis, John R. Democracy and Sport. New York: A. S. Barnes, 1941. 52 pp.

Turkin, Hy and S. C. Thompson. The Official Encyclopedia of Baseball. New York: A. S. Barnes, 1951. 451 pp.

Washington, Booker T. The Future of the American Negro. Boston: Small, Maynard, 1902. 174 pp.

Weaver, Robert B. Amusements and Sports in American Life. Chicago: University of Chicago, 1939. 195 pp.

White, Walter. How Far the Promised Land. New York: Viking Press, 1956. 238 pp.

Woodward, Comer V. The Strange Career of Jim Crow. New York: Oxford University Press, 1955. 155 pp.

B.   PERIODICAL ARTICLES

Anonymous. "The South Sees Jackie," Newsweek, XXXI (April 19, 1948), 82.

_____ "The National Game," Time, LXIII (June 14, 1954), 46.

_____ "You've Gotta Be Crazy to Hate Jackie Robinson," New Review, I, (September, 1954), 59-61.

Brown, Gertye West. "The Mighty Mite," Our Sports, I (May, 1953), 36-39.

Cohn, Howard. "The Gibson Story," American Lawn Tennis, XXXIV (July, 1950), 7.

Kahn, Roger. "What Big Leaguers Really Think of Negroes," Our Sports, I (June, 1953), 64-65.

Lardner, John. "The 50 Percent Color Line," Newsweek, XLIV (May 10, 1954), 95.

Mann, Arthur. "The Truth About the Jackie Robinson Case," Saturday Evening Post, CCXXIII (May 13, 1950), 19-20, 120-123.

Marble, Alice. "A Vital Issue," American Lawn Tennis, XXXIV (July, 1950), 14.

Meade, George P. "The Negro in Track Athletics," Scientific Monthly, LXXV (December 1952), 366-371.

Mitchell, Jonathan. "Joe Louis Never Smiles," New Republic, LXXXIV (October 9, 1935), 239.

White, Walter, "Time For a Progress Report," Saturday Review, XXXIV (September 22, 1951), 39.

Winterich, John. "Playing Ball," Saturday Review, XXVIII (November 24, 1945), 12.

C.   NEWSPAPERS

Fresno Bee, November 4, 1946 to July 7, 1957.

Los Angeles Times, August 5, 1956.

New York Times, March 1, 1920 to September 5, 1922.

_____ , May 17, 1939 to March 1, 1957.

San Francisco Chronicle, July 22, 1956.

Visalia Times-Delta, November 6, 1956.

D.   GOVERNMENT PUBLICATIONS

Congressional Record. 62nd Congress, 2nd session, 48:8 (July 1 - August 1, 1912),
    7890-9988.

Georgia.   State Law Department.   Compilation of Georgia Laws and Opinons of the Attorney
    General Relating to Segregation of the Races. Atlanta: April, 1956. 92 pp.

APPENDIX A

LETTER SENT TO SECRETARIES OF STATE OF

FOURTEEN SOUTHERN STATES

July 10, 1956

Secretary of State
[Name of State]
State Capitol
[Name of City]

Dear Sir:

For my Master's thesis in history I am attempting to compile information on the present extent of racial segregation in sports and athletic events in the United States.

I would greatly appreciate any information you can send me pertaining to legislation which [name of state] may have dealing with racial segregation at athletic events and similar activities.

My purpose is not to form an opinion or pass any judgement, but simply to ascertain the facts.

Thank you for whatever assistance you can give me in this.

Sincerely,

T. Elton Foreman
2404 Pecan Drive
Visalia, California

APPENDIX B

LETTER SENT TO DIRECTORS OF ATHLETICS

OF TWENTY SOUTHERN UNIVERSITIES

August 1, 1956

Director of Athletics
[Name of university]
[City and State]

Dear Sir:

For my Master's thesis in history I am attempting to compile information on the present extent of racial segregation in sports in the United States.

I would greatly appreciate any information you can send me pertaining to your schools' policy in regard to scheduling games with schools which may use Negro players--either on your own field or on theirs.

I would also be interested in knowing whether, in your own opinion, there has been less restriction on mixed racial athletic competition in your area in recent years than formerly, or more.

My purpose in this is not to form any opinion or pass any judgement, but simply to ascertain the facts.

Thank you for whatever assistance you can give me in this.

Sincerely,

T. Elton Foreman
2404 Pecan Drive
Visalia, California

APPENDIX C

LETTER SENT TO DIRECTORS OF ATHLETICS OF TWENTY

UNIVERSITIES OUTSIDE OF THE SOUTH

August 15, 1956

Director of Athletics
[Name of School]
[City and State]

Dear Sir:

For my Master's thesis in history I am attempting to compile information on the present extent of racial segregation in sports in the United States.

I would greatly appreciate any information you can give me on the following questions:

(1)   Does your school have any policy, official or unwritten, in regard to scheduling games with schools in areas where there might be discrimination against Negro athletes?

(2)   Has your school had any recent experience, favorable or unfavorable, in regard to mixed racial athletic competition?

(3)   Have you personally noted any trend toward more or less restriction on mixed racial athletic competition in recent years?

My purpose in this is not to form any opinion or pass any judgement, but simply to ascertain the facts.

Thank you for whatever assistance you can give me.

Sincerely,

T. Elton Foreman
2404 Pecan Drive
Visalia, California

APPENDIX D

TEXT OF LOUISIANA STATE LAW PROHIBITING MIXED RACIAL

ATHLETIC EVENTS

ACT. NO. 579

House Bill No. 1412

By: Mssrs. Gibbs, Gleason, and Percy

AN ACT

To prohibit all interracial dancing, social functions, entertainments, athletic training, games, sports or contests and other such activities, to provide for separate seating, and other facilities for whites and Negroes; to provide penalties for the violation of this Act, to provide a date on which this Act shall become effective, and to repeal all laws or parts of laws in conflict herewith.

Be it enacted by the Legislature of Louisiana:

    Section 1.   That all persons, firms, and corporations are prohibited from sponsoring, arranging, participating in, or permitting on premises under their control any dancing, social functions, entertainments, athletic training, games, sports or contests and other such activities involving personal and social contacts, in which the participants or contestants are members of the white and negro races.
    Section 2.   That at any entertainment or athletic contests, where the public is invited or may attend, the sponsors or those in control of the premises shall provide separate seating arrangements, and separate sanitary, drinking water and any other facilities for members of the white and negro races, and to mark such separate accommodations and facilities with signs printed in bold letters.
    Section 3.   That white persons are prohibited from sitting in or using any part of seating arrangements and sanitary or other facilities set apart for members of the negro race; and members of the negro race are prohibited from sitting in or using any part or seating arrangements and sanitary or other facilities set apart for white persons.
    Section 4.   Any person, firm or corporation violating the provisions of this Act shall be guilty of a misdemeanor and, upon conviction, shall be fined not less than $100.00 or more than $1,000.00 and imprisoned for not less than 60 days or more than 1 year.

Section 5.   This Act is passed in the exercise of the State Police Power to regulate public health, morals, and to maintain peace and good order in the State and shall be so construed.   This Act shall not become effective until the fifteenth (15th) day of October, 1956.   None of the provisions of this bill shall be construed to apply to religious gatherings, services or functions.

Section 6.   That any laws or parts of laws in conflict herewith be and the same are hereby repealed.

Approved by the Governor July 16, 1956.

A true copy:

    WADE O. MARTIN, JR.
    Secretary of State